Boat

COLORING BOOK FOR ADULTS

SKETCH DESIGN

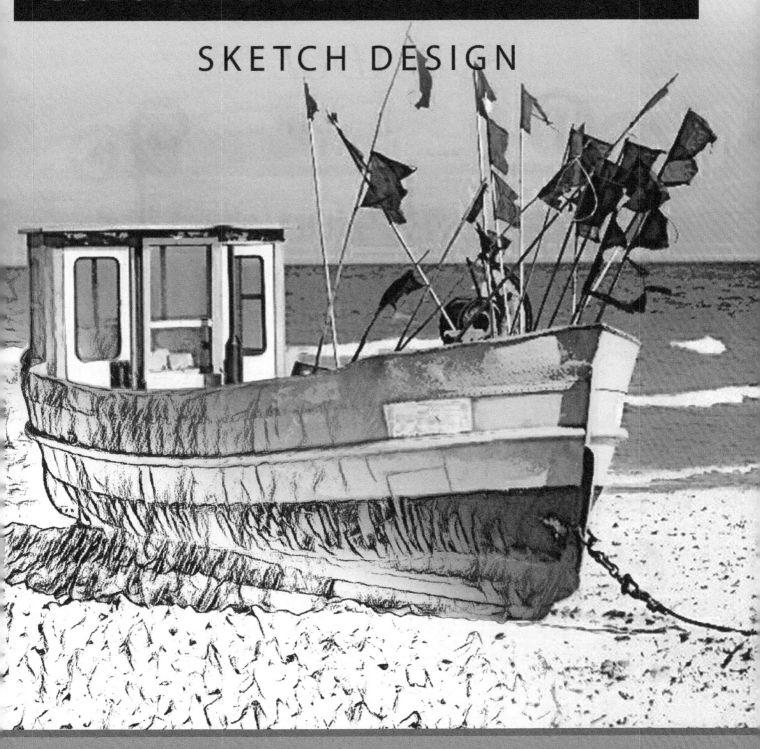

COLORING BOOKS
FOR ADULTS

This Book
belongs to

TEST YOUR COLOR

For Your
Design

For Your
Design

For Your
Design

For Your
Design

For Your
Design

For Your
Design

For Your
Design

For Your
Design

For Your
Design

For Your
Design

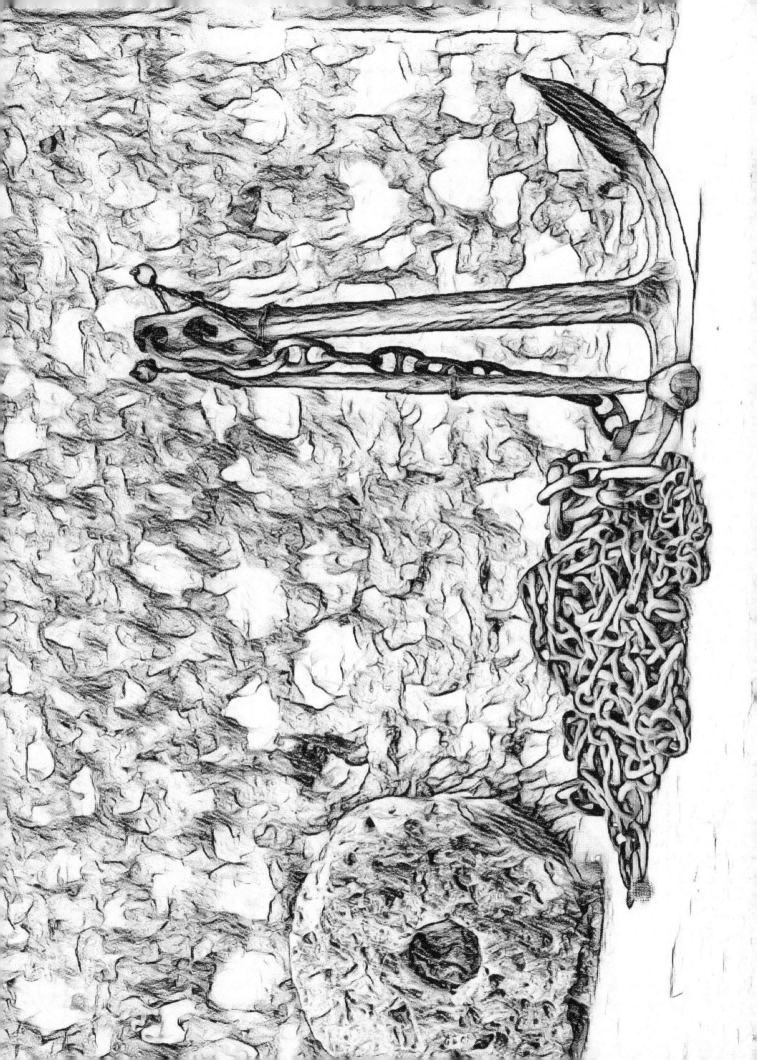

For Your
Design

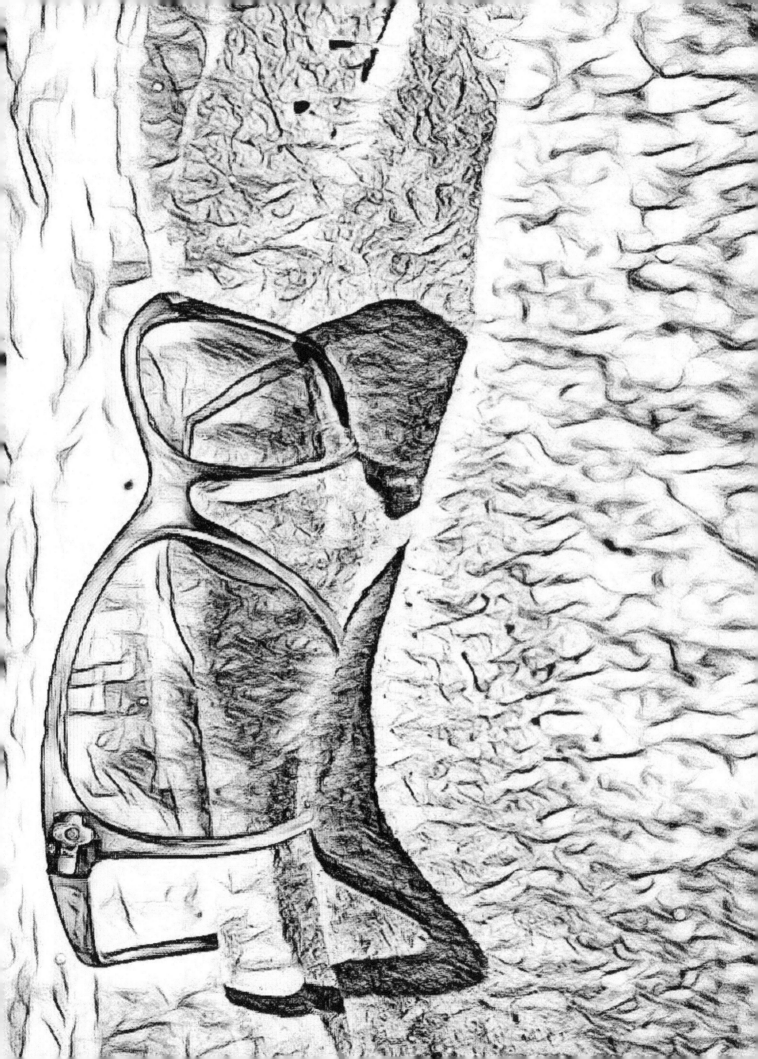

For Your
Design

For Your
Design

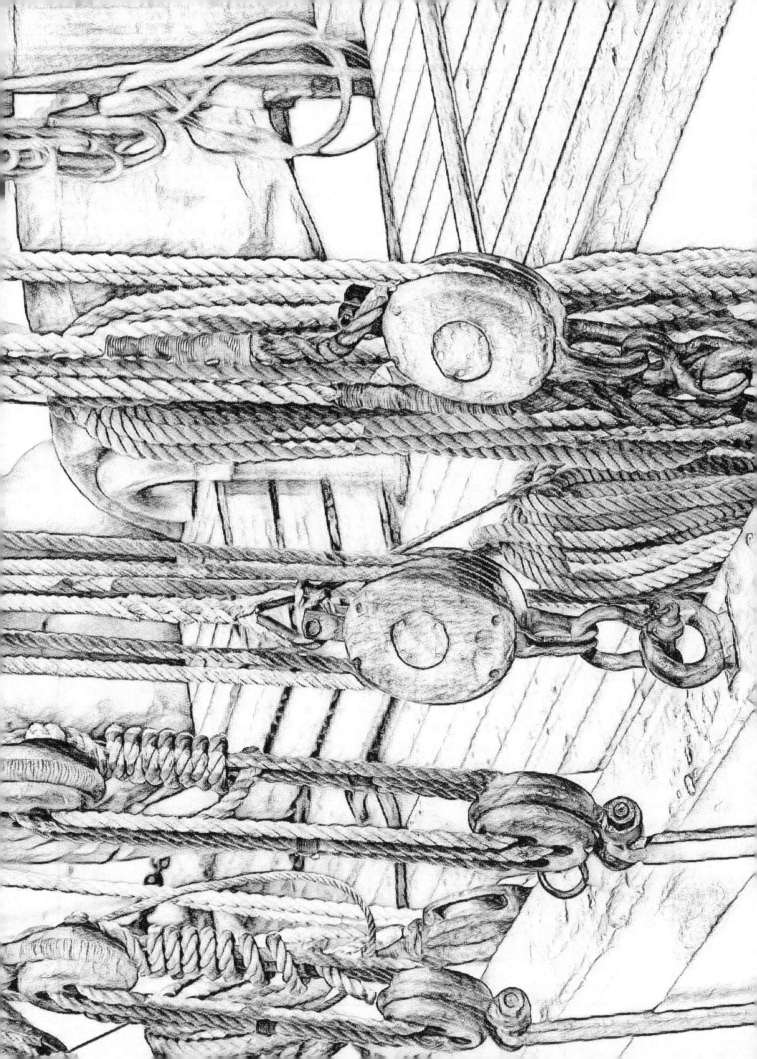

For Your
Design

For Your
Design

For Your
Design

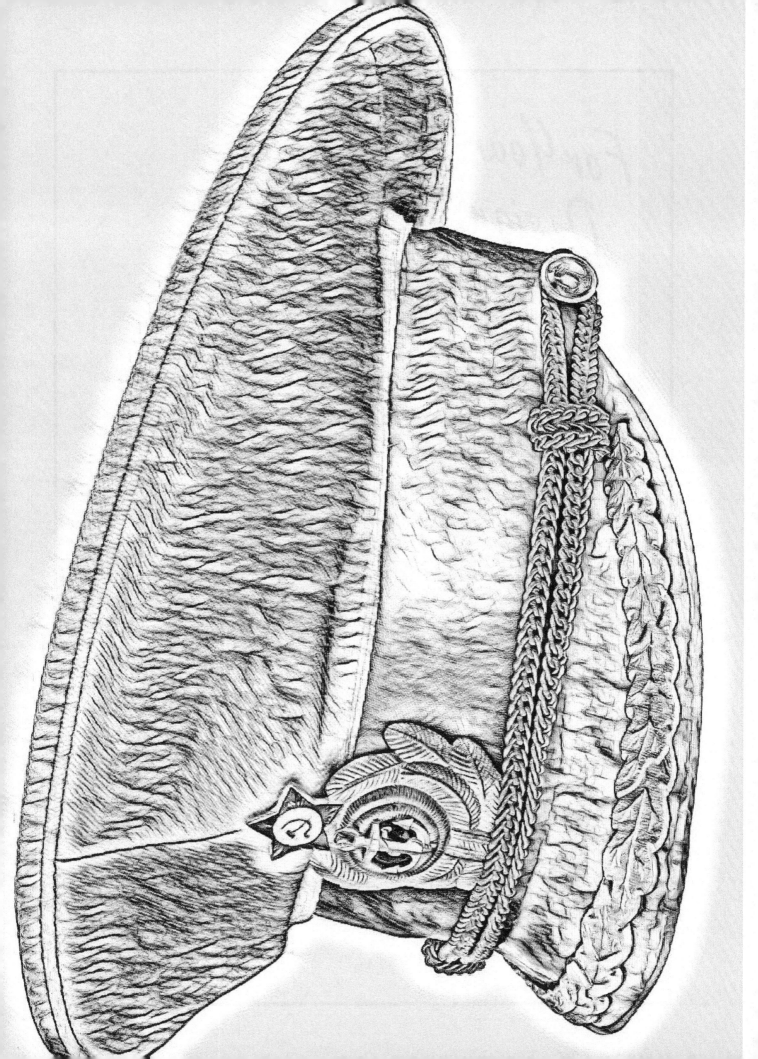

For Your
Design

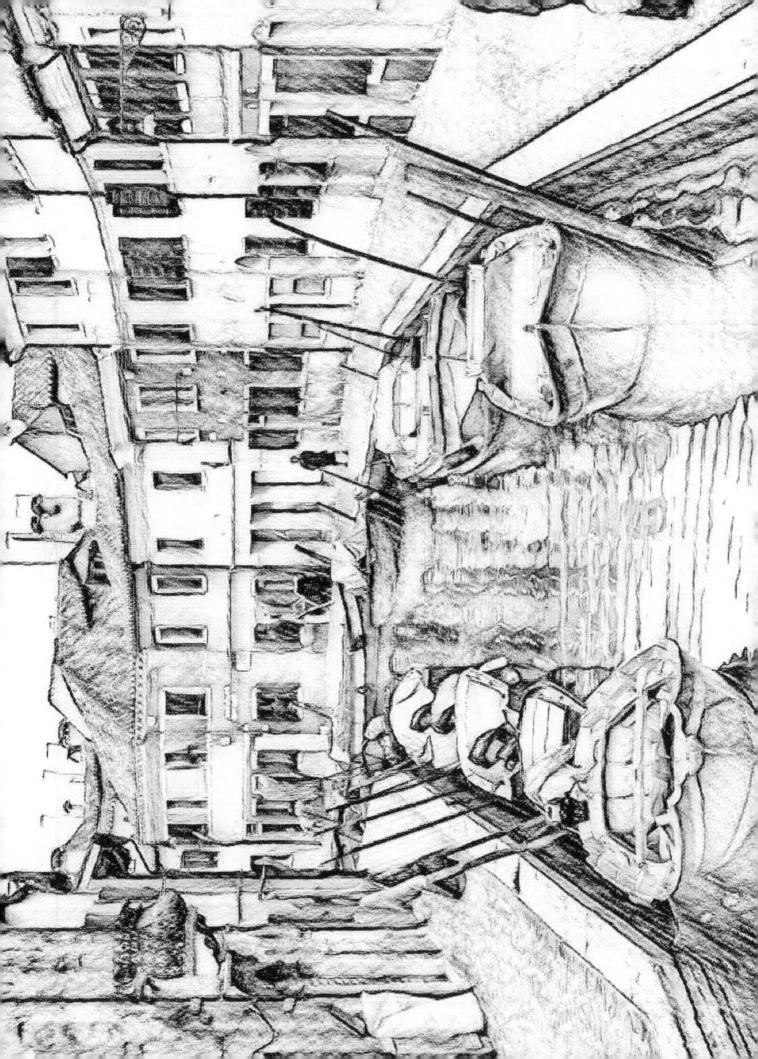

For Your
Design

For Your
Design

For Your
Design

For Your
Design

For Your
Design

Made in United States
Orlando, FL
13 July 2023

35031117R00030